Lost in the Forest

Happy House

About Wise & Wide

- A systematic 6-level English reading program based on Lexile® measures
- Diverse and interesting topics chosen from the elementary curriculums of Korea and English speaking western countries
- Well-written books in various forms including fiction stories, descriptive texts, and classics retold
- The informative but original fiction stories grab your interest, leading to the easy and clear understanding of the educational content.
- Improve thinking skills with solid after-reading activities at all levels of the series.

Wise & Wide is a 6-level English reading program that consists of 60 books and each level is systematically divided by Lexile® measures. The Lexile® Framework for Reading is the most popular reading measuring system in American formal education curriculums and many English programs. Over 20 out of 50 states in the U.S. mark Lexile® measures directly on students' final report cards and over 300 well-known publishers adopt and use Lexile® measures.

Experience many kinds of readings written by professional writers from the U.S. and England. They used interesting topics that were carefully chosen after analyzing elementary curriculums from around the world including Korea, the U.S., England, and Australia among many others. Comprehensive after-reading activities including graphic organizers, speaking tasks, and After-reading Tests are ready for you.

Levels in the series and their corresponding Lexile® measures

Level	Lexile® measures	U.S. Grade
Level 1	Below 200L	Pre K - K
Level 2	190L - 400L	Lower Grade 1
Level 3	350L - 530L	Upper Grade 1
Level 4	420L - 650L	Grade 2
Level 5	520L - 940L	Grade 3 - 4
Level 6	830L - 1070L	Grade 5 - 6

* Smart Readers: Wise & Wide level 1 is applicable to the preschool level in the U.S.

* The source of the relationship between Lexile® measures and U.S. school grades: CCSS(Common Core State Standards) FOR ENGLISH LANGUAGE ARTS, APPENDIX A (2012, which is used by 45 states in the U.S.)

Topic List

	Level 1	Level 2	Level 3	Level 4	Level 5	Level 6
Book 1	Science>Biology: The hibernation of animals Story	Science>Biology: Living and nonliving things Story	Science>Biology> Animals & the Environment: Sea otters Story	Environment> Living with nature: The diver & the persimmon tree Story	Science>Biology> Animal: Amazing animals of the Amazon Story	Science>Biology: Germs, transmitted diseases Story
Book 2	Literature> World classics: Aesop's fables Story	Literature> Traditional fairy tale: Old tales about stones Story	Social Studies> Economy: To run a business to make and save money Story	Science>Biology> Plants: Photosynthesis Story	Science>Earth science: Earth's layers, earthquakes, volcanoes, and earth's atmosphere Report	Mathematics> Sequence: The golden ratio & the Fibonacci sequence Story
Book 3	Science>Physics: How shadows are formed Story	Literature> World classics: Peter Pan Story	Science>Scientific technology: Nanobots Story	Literature>Myths: World's creation stories Story	Literature> Legend: The story of King Arthur Story	Literature>Myths: Constellation myths Story
Book 4	Literature> Traditional literature: The Talmud Story	Science>Biology> Animal: Polar bears Story	Science>Biology> Animal: Mountain gorillas Story	Social Studies> Cultural anthropology: Amazing ancient cultures of the world Story	Science> Earth science: Clouds and weather Story	Literature> Human & animals: The friendship between a girl and a horse Story
Book 5	Social Studies> Ethics: Rules in daily life Story	Science>Biology: The five senses Report	Social Studies> Cultural anthropology: Astonishing festivals Report	Art>Music: Stories from two operas Story	Social Studies> World culture & history: The Renaissance Story	Sports> Board sports: Surfing & snowboarding Story
Book 6	Social Studies> World geography & travel: Tourist attractions around the world Story	Science>Biology> Animal: Dinosaurs Story	Science> Astronomy: The solar system Story	Social Studies> People: Three great people who overcame hardships Story	Science>Scientific technology: The wonderful world of robots Report	Art>Music: Composers of the Romantic Era Report
Book 7	Science> Space science: The life of astronauts Report	Social Studies> Cultural anthropology: Mythological monsters from around the world Report	Mathematics> Elementary mathematics: Numbers, measurement, shapes and data Report	Science & Social Studies> Technology & culture: Inventions from around the world Report	Art>Works of art: Famous paintings Report	Social Studies> Human & animals: Animals in action for human Report
Book 8	Social Studies> Cultural anthropology: Various living cultures of the world Story	Art>Music: Instruments in the orchestra Story	Social Studies> Life safety: Learning and using outdoor survival skills Story	Social Studies> History: The California Gold Rush Report	Social Studies & Science> Psychology: Psychology in everyday life Story	Literature> World classics: The Merchant of Venice Story
Book 9	Social Studies> Jobs: Interviews about jobs Report	Science>Scientific technology: Developments in technology in different times Story	Social Studies> Politics>Election: Running for 3rd grade class president Story	Literature> World classics: Stories of Sherlock Holmes Story	Literature> World classics: Adrift in the Pacific Story	Social Studies> History & People: Great world leaders in history Report
Book 10	Literature>Traditional fairy tale: Eastern and Western folk tales on the same theme Story	Sports>Winter sports: Various aspects of some Winter Olympic sports Report	Literature> World classics: Short stories by O. Henry Story	Sports> Ball games: Various aspects of popular ball games Report	Social Studies> History: Famous events that changed world history Report	Art & Social Studies> Art: Stories about the creation, distribution, and preservation of paintings Report

* 10 books in each level will be published.

How to Use This Book

•Before Reading

You can easily find the topic and what kind of story you are about to read.

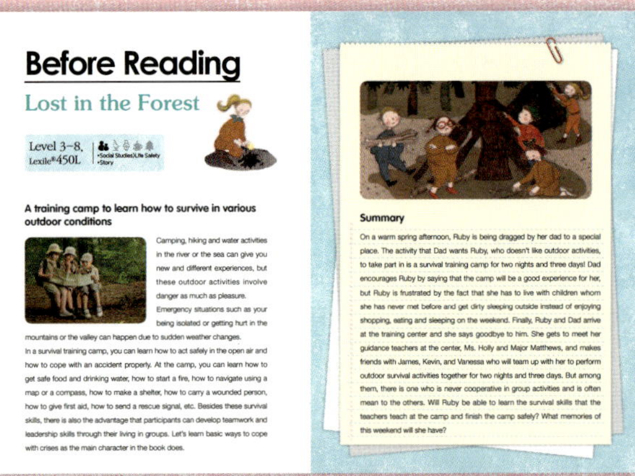

•The text

All the stories were written by professional writers from the U.S. and England, so you will read authentic and appropriate English sentences and expressions in every book in the series.

•Pop Quiz

Check out right away if you understand what you have just read by solving a pop quiz that checks your comprehension.

•Key Words

The key words and expressions on each page are listed for you to easily study them.

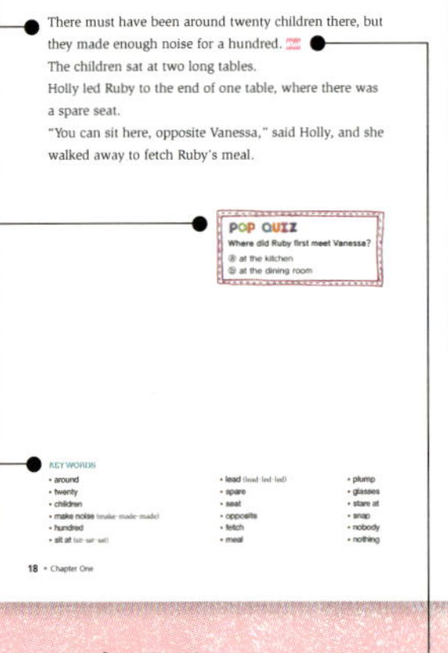

•Aha! Tips

Download free Korean explanations at *www.ihappyhouse.co.kr* for all of the sentences marked with "Aha!". These explain cultural, scientific, and economic knowledge or they deal with aspects of English such as grammatical structures or idiomatic expressions. There are lots of "Aha! Tips" to help you understand the text.

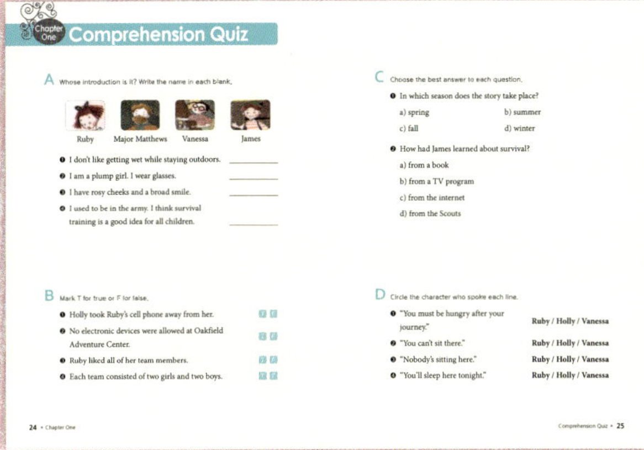

•Comprehension Quiz

After reading one chapter, solve various questions to find out if you fully understand the content.

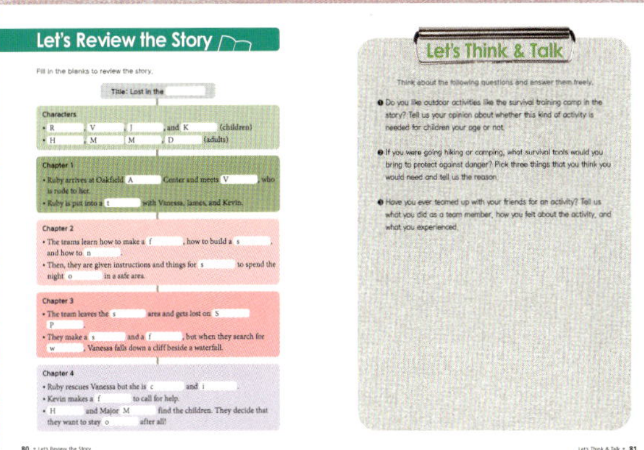

•Let's Review the Story /
•Let's Think & Talk

Fill in the blanks in the organizer to summarize the whole story. Express your own thinking and feelings about the story by answering the questions. You can build up logic and reasoning skills for your essay examinations in the future.

Appendix

Audio CD

In the CD audio book form, the texts are read vividly by American professional voice actors.
(MP3 files downloaded for free)

After-reading Test

Solve an additionally provided After-reading Test for each book.

The Korean translation, Answer Keys, a Word Quiz, a Word List, and Aha! Tips for each book

You can download them for free at *www.ihappyhouse.co.kr* or *www.darakwon.co.kr*

Before Reading

Lost in the Forest

A training camp to learn how to survive in various outdoor conditions

Camping, hiking and water activities in the river or the sea can give you new and different experiences, but these outdoor activities involve danger as much as pleasure. Emergency situations such as your being isolated or getting hurt in the mountains or the valley can happen due to sudden weather changes.

In a survival training camp, you can learn how to act safely in the open air and how to cope with an accident properly. At the camp, you can learn how to get safe food and drinking water, how to start a fire, how to navigate using a map or a compass, how to make a shelter, how to carry a wounded person, how to give first aid, how to send a rescue signal, etc. Besides these survival skills, there is also the advantage that participants can develop teamwork and leadership skills through their living in groups. Let's learn basic ways to cope with crises as the main character in the book does.

Summary

On a warm spring afternoon, Ruby is being dragged by her dad to a special place. The activity that Dad wants Ruby, who doesn't like outdoor activities, to take part in is a survival training camp for two nights and three days! Dad encourages Ruby by saying that the camp will be a good experience for her, but Ruby is frustrated by the fact that she has to live with children whom she has never met before and get dirty sleeping outside instead of enjoying shopping, eating and sleeping on the weekend. Finally, Ruby and Dad arrive at the training center and she says goodbye to him. She gets to meet her guidance teachers at the center, Ms. Holly and Major Matthews, and makes friends with James, Kevin, and Vanessa who will team up with her to perform outdoor survival activities together for two nights and three days. But among them, there is one who is never cooperative in group activities and is often mean to the others. Will Ruby be able to learn the survival skills that the teachers teach at the camp and finish the camp safely? What memories of this weekend will she have?

Lost in the Forest

Lost in the Forest

A Weekend Away

"But why do I have to go?"

Ruby folded her arms and scowled.

"I want to go shopping with Mom.

I don't want to spend the weekend getting wet and

dirty."

"It'll be good for you," said Dad.

"You don't get outdoors enough.

Anyway, it's not that cold.

It's spring, after all, and they'll give you all the right

clothes to wear."

KEY WORDS

- weekend
- away
- **have to + *Verb*** (have-had-had)
- **fold one's arms** (*cf.* fold)
- **scowl**
- **want to + *Verb***
- **go shopping** (go-went-gone)
- **spend** (spend-spent-spent)
- **get wet** (*cf.* wet)

- dirty
- be good for
- **outdoors** (*cf.* outdoor)
- **enough**
- anyway
- after all
- right
- clothes
- **wear** (wear-wore-worn)

At last, they turned into a narrow lane.

A sign at the entrance said, *Oakfield Adventure Center.*

At the end of the lane was a low, stone building.

Beyond it were fields, which gave way to hills and then

mountains.

KEY WORDS

- at last
- turn
- narrow
- lane
- sign
- entrance

- adventure
- at the end of
- low
- stone
- building
- beyond

- field
- give way to (*cf.* way)
- hill
- then
- mountain

The tops of all the mountains were cloaked in mist.

A thick forest covered the tallest mountain.

"That's Survivor's Peak beyond those hills," said Dad.

"You won't be going up there.

It's very dangerous.

There are steep cliffs.

People have been killed falling down them."

"Why is it called Survivor's Peak?" asked Ruby.

"A team of climbers had an accident there," said Dad.

"There was only one survivor."

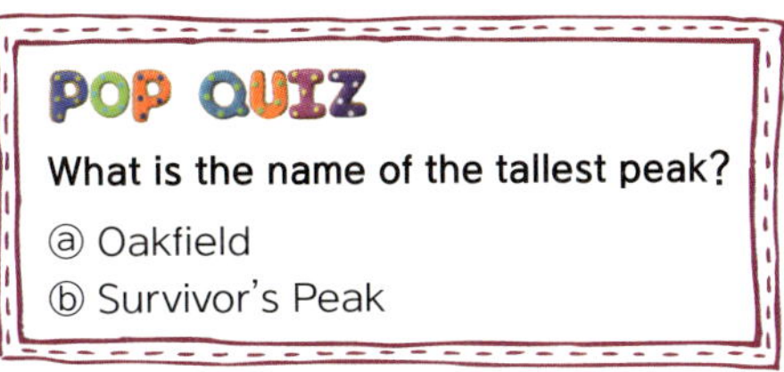

KEY WORDS

- top
- cloak
- mist
- thick
- forest
- cover
- tallest
- survivor
- peak
- won't
- go up
- dangerous
- steep
- cliff
- fall down (fall-fell-fallen)
- call
- a team of
- climber (*cf.* climb)
- accident
- only

A young woman came out of the building.

Her blonde hair was tied back in a ponytail.

"You must be Ruby!" she exclaimed.

"Welcome to Oakfield.

My name is Holly.

We've been expecting you."

"It's great to meet you, Holly," said Dad, getting out of the car to shake Holly's hand.

Ruby mumbled a quick hello.

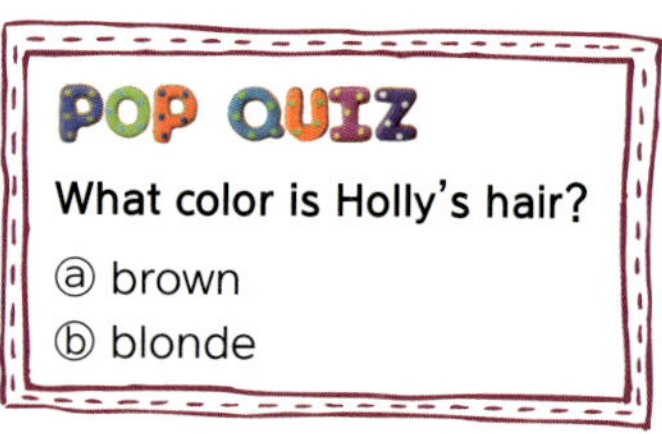

KEY WORDS

- **come out of** (come-came-come)
- **blonde**
- **hair**
- **tie**
- **ponytail**
- **must**
- **exclaim**
- **welcome to**
- **expect**
- **get out of** (get-got-gotten)
- **shake one's hand** (shake-shook-shaken) (*cf.* shake / hand)
- **mumble**
- **quick**

"Come on in," said Holly.

"I'll introduce you to your camp mates."

Ruby got out of the car slowly.

Dad unloaded her bags and gave her a quick hug.

Then, he got back into the car and drove away.

Ruby wanted to run after him.

Instead, she followed Holly indoors.

KEY WORDS

- Come on in.
- introduce A to B
- camp
- mate
- unload

- bag
- hug
- get back into
- drive away
  (drive-drove-driven)

- run after (run-ran-run)
- instead
- follow
- indoors (↔ outdoors)

They went through a large hallway.

Then, they turned left into a corridor that had doors on both sides.

"This is your bedroom," explained Holly, opening one of the doors.

There were two sets of bunk beds against the walls.

"You'll sleep in here with three other girls," said Holly.

"Well, you'll sleep here tonight.

Tomorrow, you'll be sleeping outdoors."

Ruby couldn't believe her ears.

This room looked bad enough, but there was no way she was going to sleep outdoors. **Aha!**

Not in a million years!

Holly kept on smiling.

"The others have just started dinner. You must be hungry after your journey."

Ruby wasn't hungry at all; in fact, she felt a little sick. But she followed Holly back down the corridor, across the hallway and into a large, noisy dining room.

KEY WORDS

- **go through** (*cf.* through)
- **hallway** (= corridor)
- **turn left**
- **both**
- **side**
- **explain**
- **a set of**
- **bunk bed**
- **other**
- **tomorrow**
- **believe**
- **look**
- **(there is) no way**
- **not in a million years**
- **keep on +** *Verb***-ing** (keep-kept-kept)
- **hungry**
- **journey**
- **not ~ at all**
- **in fact**
- **feel sick** (feel-felt-felt)
- **across**
- **noisy** (*cf.* noise)
- **dining room**

There must have been around twenty children there, but they made enough noise for a hundred. **Aha!**

The children sat at two long tables.

Holly led Ruby to the end of one table, where there was a spare seat.

"You can sit here, opposite Vanessa," said Holly, and she walked away to fetch Ruby's meal.

KEY WORDS

- around
- twenty
- children
- make noise (make-made-made)
- hundred
- sit at (sit-sat-sat)

- lead (lead-led-led)
- spare
- seat
- opposite
- fetch
- meal

- plump
- glasses
- stare at
- snap
- nobody
- nothing

Ruby sat down.

Vanessa, a plump girl with glasses, stared at her.

"You can't sit there," she snapped.

"Why not? Nobody's sitting here," said Ruby.

Vanessa said nothing.

She just scowled and went back to her meal.

After dinner, everyone gathered in the main meeting room.

Ruby slid her cell phone from her pocket and began to text her mom.

Come and get me, she wrote. *It's horrible here.*

She was just about to press "send" when a hand swooped down from behind her.

"No phones, tablets, computers or other electronic devices allowed," said a male voice.

"You can have it back after the weekend."

KEY WORDS

- **gather**
- **main**
- **meeting room**
- **slide** (slide-slid-slid)
- **cell phone**
- **begin** (begin-began-begun)
- **text**
- **write** (write-wrote-written)
- **horrible**
- **be about to** + *Verb*
- **press**

- **swoop**
- **tablet**
- **electronic**
- **device**
- **allowed** (*cf.* allow)
- **male**
- **voice**
- **have a chance to** + *Verb*
- **protest**
- **take away** (take-took-taken)
- **stand** (stand-stood-stood)

- **front**
- **boom**
- **major**
- **learn about**
- **survival**
- **develop**
- **confidence**
- **courage**
- **each**
- **consist of**

Before Ruby had a chance to protest, her phone was
taken away.

The man went and stood at the front.

"Good evening, everyone!" he boomed.

"My name is Major Matthews.

You are here to learn about survival.

You are also here to develop your own confidence and
courage.

You will work in teams of four.

Each team will consist of two girls and two boys."

Major Matthews read out the names.

Ruby was put with two boys called James and Kevin. **Aha!**

James seemed friendly enough.

He had rosy cheeks and a broad smile.

"I know how to do everything," said James.

"I've done everything before, in the Scouts."

Kevin didn't say anything.

He kept his head down and wouldn't look at anyone.

"And the fourth member of your team is…" said Major Matthews.

Ruby groaned as the name was read out.

"…Vanessa!"

Comprehension Quiz

A Whose introduction is it? Write the name in each blank.

Ruby

Major Matthews

Vanessa

James

❶ I don't like getting wet while staying outdoors. ____________

❷ I am a plump girl. I wear glasses. ____________

❸ I have rosy cheeks and a broad smile. ____________

❹ I used to be in the army. I think survival
training is a good idea for all children. ____________

B Mark T for true or F for false.

❶ Holly took Ruby's cell phone away from her. T F

❷ No electronic devices were allowed at Oakfield
Adventure Center. T F

❸ Ruby liked all of her team members. T F

❹ Each team consisted of two girls and two boys. T F

 Choose the best answer to each question.

❶ In which season does the story take place?

    a) spring   b) summer

    c) fall   d) winter

❷ How had James learned about survival?

    a) from a book

    b) from a TV program

    c) from the internet

    d) from the Scouts

D Circle the character who spoke each line.

❶ "You must be hungry after your journey."   **Ruby / Holly / Vanessa**

❷ "You can't sit there."   **Ruby / Holly / Vanessa**

❸ "Nobody's sitting here."   **Ruby / Holly / Vanessa**

❹ "You'll sleep here tonight."   **Ruby / Holly / Vanessa**

Chapter Two

Survival Skills

The next morning, the team learned how to make a fire and cook on it.

The first task was to collect fuel for the fire.

There were plenty of trees around the center.

It was easy to find sticks and leaves.

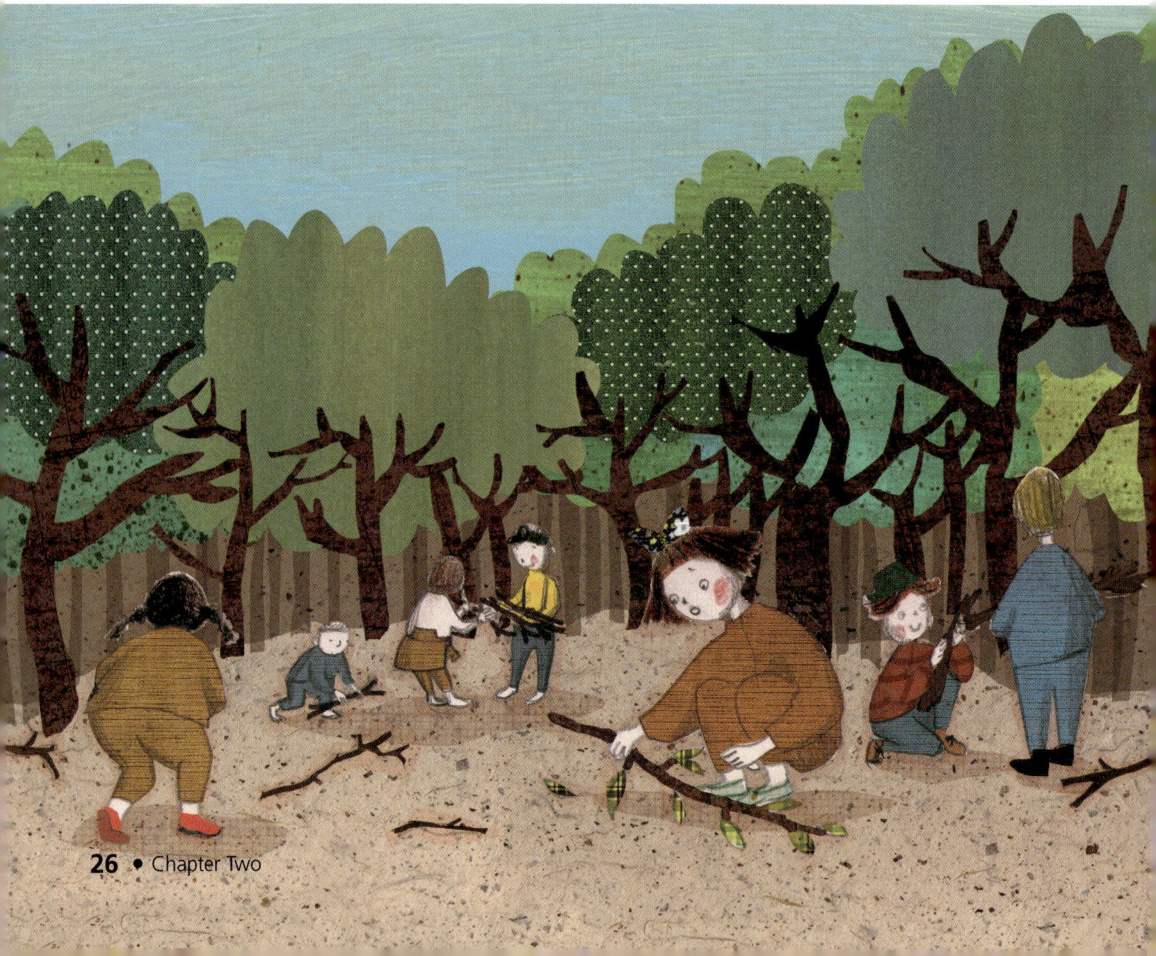

"You need dry sticks that break when you bend them,"
said Holly.
"If they are too green and damp, they won't burn
easily. **Aha!**
If they do burn, they will produce a lot of smoke."
They found enough dry sticks for a fire.
Holly showed them how to build
the sticks up in a cone shape.
"That means there will be
plenty of oxygen," she said.
"It will help the fire to burn."

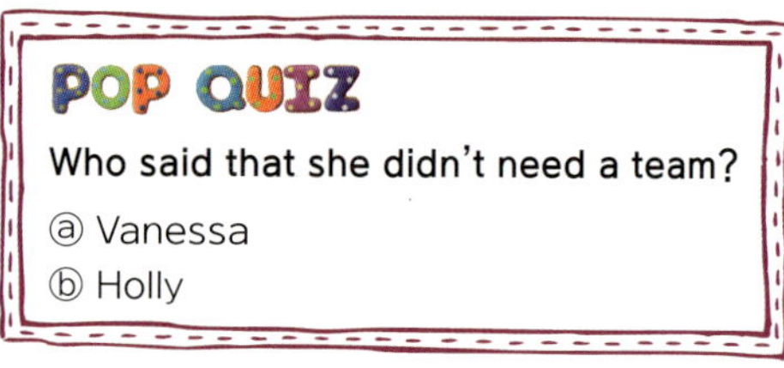

Vanessa tried, but the sticks fell down. She kicked them angrily.

"Vanessa," said Holly with a warning in her voice. "There's no need to behave like that. When it comes to survival, you need to work as a team. Your life could depend on it."

"I don't need a team," snapped Vanessa. "I'd rather do it by myself."

POP QUIZ

Who said that she didn't need a team?
ⓐ Vanessa
ⓑ Holly

KEY WORDS

- try
- kick
- angrily
- warning (*cf.* warn)
- behave
- when it comes to
- as
- life
- depend on
- would rather
- by oneself
- be good at
- Well done.
- glance at
- shyly
- give a quick smile
  (give-gave-given)
- look away
- toward
- distant
- even
- forbidding
- be hidden in
  (*cf.* hide (hide-hid-hidden))
- cloud

Kevin was good at building the sticks in just the right
way.

"Well done," said Ruby.

Kevin glanced at her shyly and gave a quick smile.

Then, he looked away again, toward the distant
Survivor's Peak.

It looked even more forbidding than it had this morning.

The top was now hidden in clouds.

The children learned about the fire triangle. 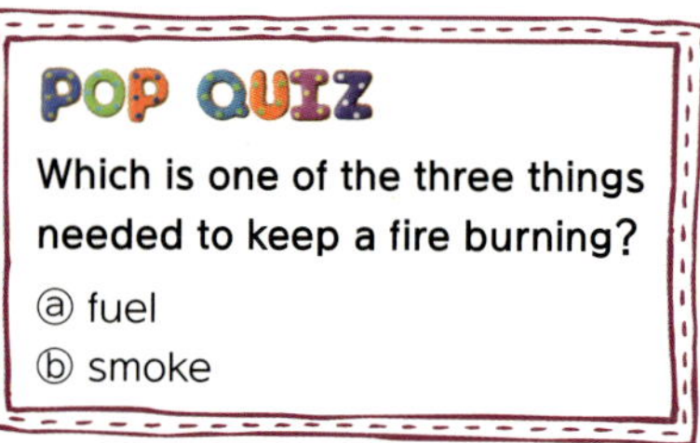

They were the three things needed to keep a fire burning.

"What are they?" demanded Holly.

"Fuel," said Vanessa.

"Oxygen," said James.

"Heat," said Ruby.

Kevin said nothing, but he listened intently.

POP QUIZ

Which is one of the three things needed to keep a fire burning?

ⓐ fuel
ⓑ smoke

KEY WORDS

- triangle
- demand
- heat
- listen
- intently
- light (light-lit-lit)

- use
- firesteel (= firestriker)
- be made of
- plastic
- bit (= piece)
- metal

- scrape
- spark
- none
- useless
- grumble
- either

"Now you need to light it using the firesteel."

Holly handed one to Ruby.

It was made of plastic and two bits of metal.

Holly showed her how to scrape one piece of metal against another to make a spark.

Ruby made spark after spark, but none of them lit the sticks.

"You're useless," grumbled Vanessa.

"You try, then," said Ruby.

But Vanessa couldn't light it either.

"We need something more flammable," said Holly.
She handed a small tub of petroleum jelly to Kevin. **Aha!**
He followed her instructions and smeared it onto a piece
of cotton wool.

▲ petroleum jelly

Kevin sparked the firesteel onto
the piece of cotton wool covered
in petroleum jelly.
It lit at once, and began to burn.
Ruby smiled, enjoying the warmth
on her face.

If it wasn't for Vanessa, this would be quite fun, she
thought to herself.

KEY WORDS

- flammable
- a tub of
- petroleum jelly (*cf*. petroleum)
- instruction
- smear
- a piece of
- cotton wool
- covered in
- at once
- warmth

- if it wasn't[weren't] for
- quite
- fun
- think to oneself (think-thought-thought)
- second half
- shelter
- branch
- lean A against B
- trunk
- space

The second half of the morning was spent building
shelters.

They had to find branches.

They leaned the branches against a tree trunk or a wall.

This made a dry space where people could sleep.

But the branches kept falling down.

The children also learned to navigate, using a map and a compass.

By the end of the morning, clouds were gathering.

It looked as though it would start raining soon.

Ruby's heart sank when she thought of the night ahead.

That afternoon, Major Matthews
gathered everyone together.
"You've spent the morning
learning survival and navigation
skills," he said.
"Tonight you will use them for real.
Each team will sleep outside.

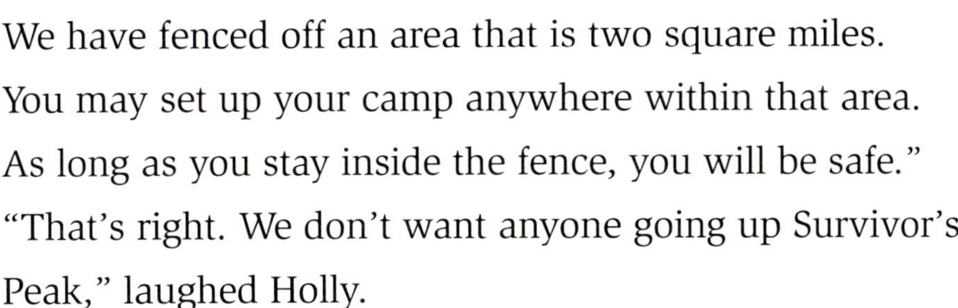

We have fenced off an area that is two square miles.
You may set up your camp anywhere within that area.
As long as you stay inside the fence, you will be safe."
"That's right. We don't want anyone going up Survivor's
Peak," laughed Holly.
"We want you all back in one piece!"

POP QUIZ

Match the two sides to complete each sentence.

ⓐ They spent the first half of the morning ·   · ① building shelters.
ⓑ They spent the second half of the morning ·   · ② making fires.

KEY WORDS

- for real
- fence off (cf. fence)
- area
- square
- mile

- may
- set up (set-set-set)
- anywhere
- within
- as long as

- stay
- inside
- safe
- laugh
- in one piece

"There will be several adults patrolling the safe area,"
the major went on.

"If there is an emergency, use your whistle."

He explained that there was a special signal.

It meant, "Help!"

It was an international distress signal. 

All over the world, people understood it.

"Blow on your whistle six times," said the major.

"Then, stop and listen.

A nearby adult will blow his or her whistle three times.

You will know that help is coming."

KEY WORDS

- several
- adult
- patrol
- go on
- emergency
- whistle
- signal
- international
- distress

- all over the world
- understand
  (understand-understood-understood)
- blow
- nearby
- backpack
- contain
- waterproof
- clothing

Each team was given four backpacks.
All the backpacks contained waterproof clothing.
One of them contained a firesteel, cotton wool,
and petroleum jelly.

It also contained water purification tablets.

"Do not drink water from a river," warned the major.

"It contains germs that can make you ill.

You must put a tablet in the water.

Leave it for at least thirty minutes.

Then, the water will be safe to drink."

KEY WORDS

- **purification tablet** (*cf*. purification)
- **drink** (drink-drank-drunk)
- **germ**
- **ill**
- **leave** (leave-left-left)
- **at least**

The teams were given a flashlight.

They were also given a large orange bag made of thick plastic.

Survival bag was printed on it.

James folded it into the size of a sheet of paper.

He gave it to Ruby, and she tucked it into her backpack.

They were given some packets of freeze-dried chicken and pasta. 

They would have to add water to them.

Then, they would be able to eat them.

KEY WORDS

- flashlight
- survival bag
- be printed on
- size

- a sheet of
- tuck
- packet
- freeze-dried

- pasta
- add
- be able to + *Verb*

Ruby, Kevin, and Vanessa each carried a backpack.

James carried the fourth backpack. **Aha!**

It contained the fire-making things.

It also contained the water purification tablets.

Ruby's team was the first to leave.

"You must find three checkpoints before you set up

camp," said Holly.

"This is to test your navigation skills.

I will go ahead of you and wait at the first checkpoint.

Blow your whistle if you get lost."

Holly strode away.

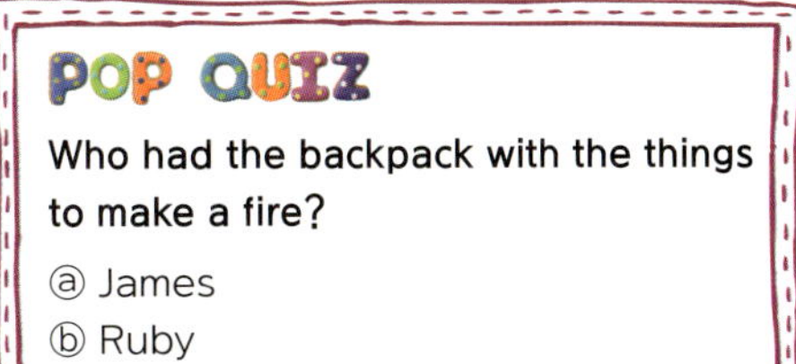

KEY WORDS

- carry
- checkpoint
- test

- go ahead
- wait
- get lost

- stride away
  (stride-strode-strode)

Comprehension Quiz

A Circle the right word for each underlined part.

❶ Water from a river may contain (<u>tablets / signals / germs</u>) that can make you ill.

❷ To make the water pure, you must put in a special (<u>tablet / signal / distress</u>).

❸ The water must be left for at least (<u>ten / twenty / thirty</u>) minutes before drinking it.

❹ A survival bag is usually made from (<u>green / orange / black</u>) plastic.

B Mark T for true or F for false.

❶ Ruby told Vanessa that she was useless at lighting the fire.   T F

❷ Ruby could not make a spark with the firesteel.   T F

❸ The firesteel was made of plastic and two bits of metal.   T F

❹ Kevin could light the fire.   T F

C Choose the best answer to each question.

❶ Why do the sticks need to be built into a cone shape?

    a) to stop them from falling down

    b) to allow oxygen into the fire

    c) to make the smoke go upward

    d) to stop the fire from burning too quickly

❷ What did Holly ask the team to find before they set up camp?

    a) three checkpoints

    b) a river

    c) two types of fuel for the fire

    d) the fence at the edge of the safe area

D Put the following sentences in the correct order of starting a fire using a firesteel.

❶ Spark the firesteel onto the cotton wool.

❷ Build the sticks into a cone shape.

❸ Smear petroleum jelly onto cotton wool.

❹ Find some dry sticks.

________ → ________ → ________ → ________

Chapter Three

Fear in the Fog

Ruby was quite good at using the map.
She had listened carefully that morning.
She knew which way to go.
But, after a few minutes, Vanessa snatched it from her hands.

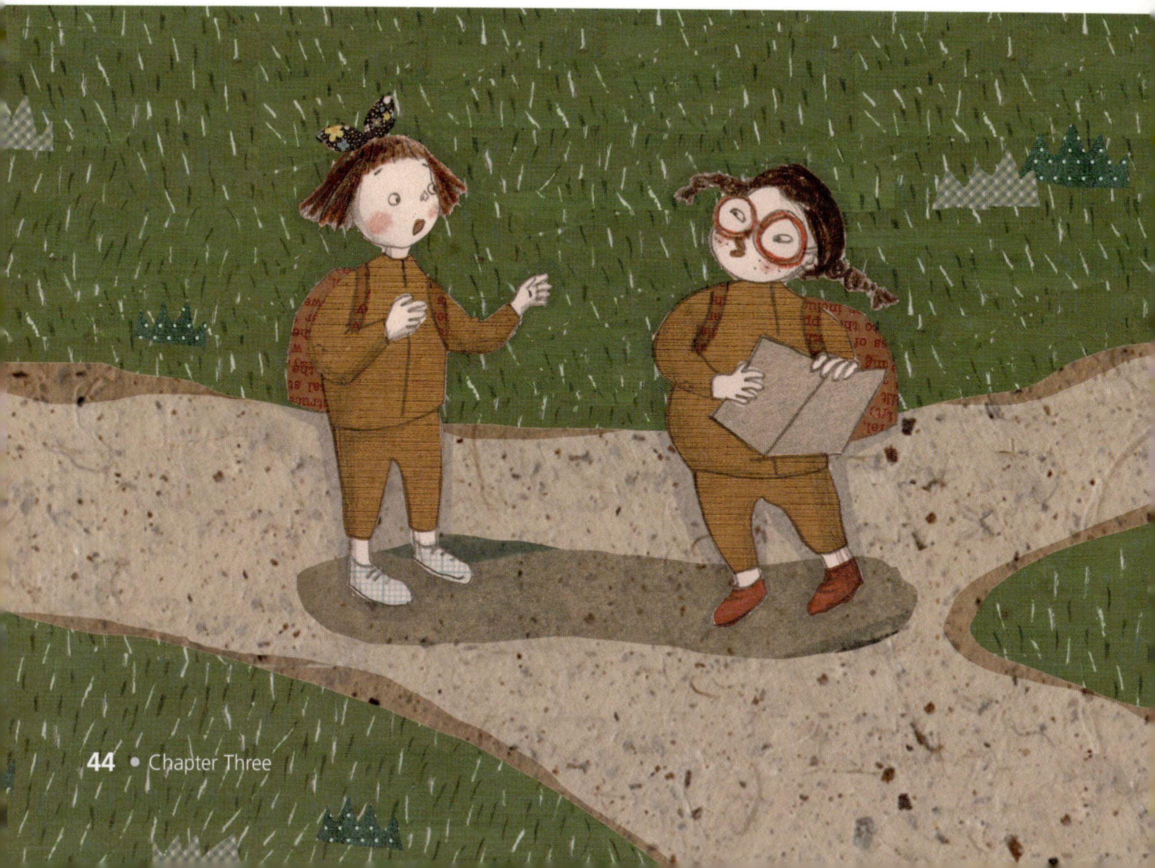

"I'm the leader," she said.

"James is my deputy."

James nodded reluctantly.

"OK," he said.

"What about Kevin and me?" asked Ruby.

But Vanessa wasn't listening.

She marched away, with James trotting after her. 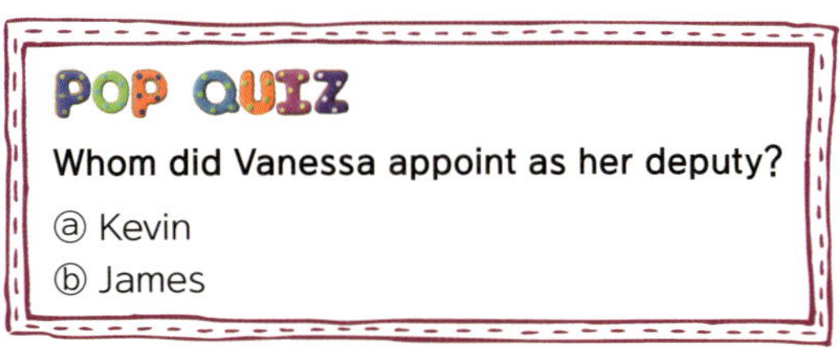

"I think she's going the wrong way," muttered Ruby as she went after them.

Kevin said nothing.

KEY WORDS

- fear
- fog
- carefully
- a few
- snatch

- leader
- deputy
- nod
- reluctantly
- what about ~?

- march
- trot
- wrong
- mutter
- go after

The children walked for about thirty minutes.

A thick, gray fog settled around them.

It covered everything.

"We should have reached the first checkpoint by now,"
said James.

"Where are we?"

For the first time that weekend, Vanessa looked uncertain.

KEY WORDS

- gray
- settle
- should have + *p.p.*
  (*cf.* should)
- reach
- by now
- for the first time
- uncertain (↔ certain)

"I don't know," she admitted.

They all looked around, but they couldn't see anything because of the fog.

"Let's blow the whistle for help," suggested Ruby.

"That's for emergencies," snapped Vanessa.

"Don't be such a baby."

KEY WORDS

- admit
- look around
- because of
- let's + *Verb*
- suggest
- such

After a while, they came to a fence.

"This must be the edge of the safe area," said James.

Vanessa climbed over it.

"Wait!" said Ruby.

"We're not allowed over there."

"So you are a baby," said Vanessa.

"Don't you want to do proper survival training?

Who wants adults spying on us all the time?"

James went pink. "I don't," he said, although he didn't sound convinced.

Kevin shook his head violently.

Ruby wasn't sure whether he was saying that they shouldn't pass the fence, or that he didn't want adults spying on him.

But she didn't want to be the only one who was scared. "Oh, all right," she sighed.

After all, they only had to whistle and help would come. They could find a good place to camp and make a fire.

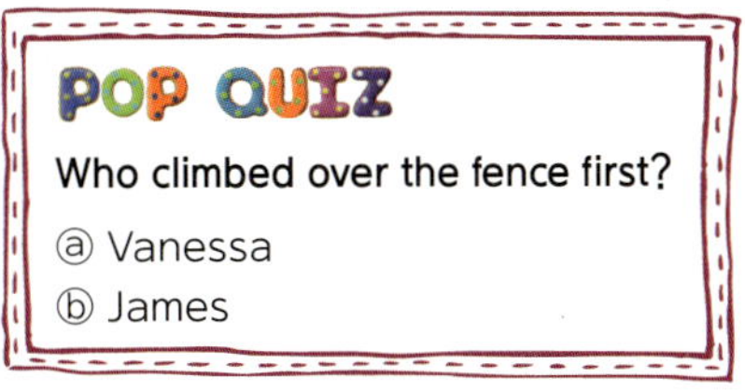

KEY WORDS

- after a while (*cf.* while)
- come to
- edge
- over there
- proper
- survival training
- spy on
- all the time
- go pink
- although
- sound
- convinced
- shake one's head
- violently
- be sure
- whether
- pass
- scared
- all right
- sigh

A steady rain began to fall.

The team walked on, looking for a good place to camp.

Ruby got her foot stuck in a sticky, muddy bog.

James took off his backpack to pull her out and they all set off again.

KEY WORDS

- **steady rain** (*cf.* steady)
- **look for**
- **get stuck** (*cf.* stuck)
- **sticky**
- **muddy**
- **bog**
- **take off**
- **pull out** (*cf.* pull)
- **set off**

After a while, Ruby realized that they were going uphill,
through a forest.

The way became steeper and steeper. **Aha!**

"Let's go back," said James.

"I want to go back to the fence."

They turned around, but the fog was too thick.

They couldn't see which way to go.

"Wait a minute," said Ruby.

"There's only one hill that has trees on it."

"Survivor's Peak!" gasped Vanessa.

POP QUIZ

How did the main characters know that they
were on Survivor's Peak?

ⓐ They could see grass around them.
ⓑ They could see trees around them.

KEY WORDS

- realize
- go uphill
- go back
- turn around
- gasp

Vanessa stepped closer to Ruby.

"What if we walk straight off the edge of a cliff?"

"Let's blow the whistle," said Ruby.

This time, Vanessa agreed.

"Who has it?" she said.

"It's in my backpack…" said James, but his face went white.

"Oh, no! I took it off to help Ruby in the bog, and I left it there!"

Together, they raised their voices and shouted.

They shouted and shouted, but there was no answering cry.

They had been out so long by now that night was creeping up on them.

"What shall we do?" whimpered Vanessa.

She had crept so close to Ruby that their arms were almost touching.

"I'm scared."

"We'll make a shelter and a fire," said Ruby, firmly.

"We can't make a fire," said James.

"The firesteel is in my backpack."

KEY WORDS

▪ step	▪ go white	▪ **creep** (creep-crept-crept)
▪ closer	▪ raise	▪ **shall** + *Verb*
▪ what if ~?	▪ shout	▪ whimper
▪ straight off	▪ answering	▪ touch
▪ agree (↔ disagree)	▪ cry	▪ **firmly** (*cf.* firm)

Kevin smiled and tapped Ruby on the shoulder.

He slid something out of his pocket.

A firesteel!

But it was no use without cotton wool and petroleum jelly.

"Wait," said Vanessa.

"I have some lip balm.

Let's try that."

James pulled some of the filling out of his coat.

They gathered sticks to make a fire and smeared lip balm on the coat filling.

Kevin managed to light it the first time!

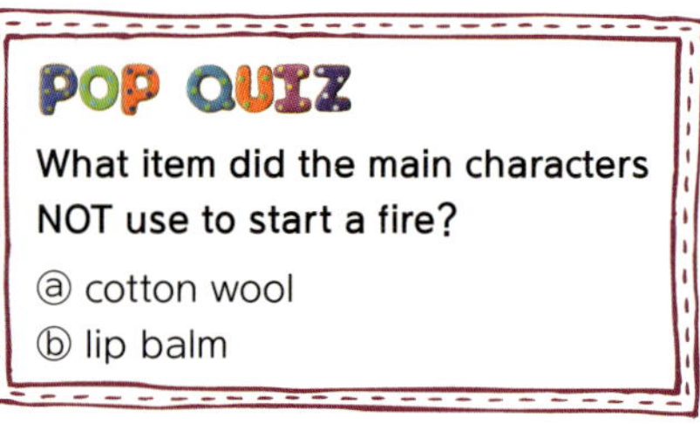

KEY WORDS

- tap A on
- shoulder
- be no use

- without
- lip balm
- filling

- coat
- manage to + *Verb*

"Now we need a shelter," said Ruby.

Together, the four of them dragged branches toward
a tree trunk.

They laid the orange survival bag on the ground.

Then, they leaned the branches against the trunk.

Vanessa found some ferns and laid them across the
branches.

They huddled next to their shelter, close to the fire.

"I'm hungry," said James.

"At least we've still got the food.

Let's eat it."

"We need some water then," said Ruby.

"Who's got the purification tablets?"

"They were in my backpack too," said James.

"Then we'll have to purify the water another way," said
Ruby.

"Remember what we were told this morning?"

James nodded.

"Boil the water over the fire and keep it boiling for five
minutes." 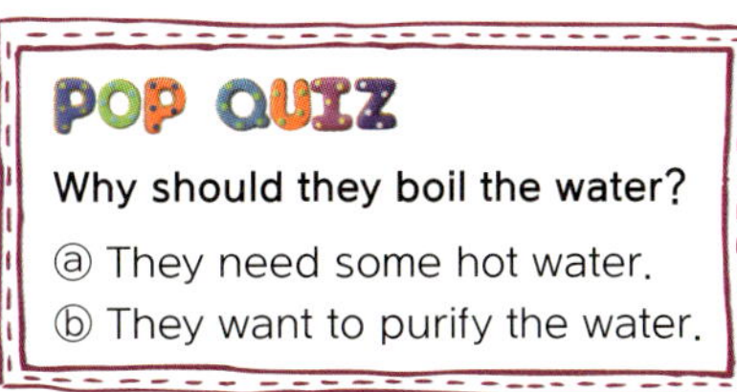

KEY WORDS

- drag
- lay (lay-laid-laid)
- ground
- fern
- huddle
- next to
- still
- purify
- (in) another way
- remember
- boil
- over the fire

So the next task was to find some water.

"It's my fault we're here," said Vanessa.

"I'll go."

Ruby listened.

She thought she heard a very faint rush of water. **Aha!**

"I'll come with you," she said.

"It's too dangerous to go alone."

She took the flashlight from her backpack.

The fog was beginning to lift now.

The girls could see a few stars in the sky.

The flashlight allowed them to see their way to the edge of a waterfall.

KEY WORDS

- fault
- hear (hear-heard-heard)
- faint
- rush
- alone
- lift

- waterfall
- below
- tumble
- careful
- slip
- a patch of

- moss
- piercing
- scream
- forward

About five meters below them, the water rushed and
tumbled into a river.

"Be careful," warned Ruby.

But it was too late.

Vanessa's foot slipped on a patch of wet moss.

With a piercing scream, she fell forward, over the edge
of the waterfall.

Comprehension Quiz

A Match each character and his or her belongings correctly.

❶ Vanessa •   • a) coat filling

❷ Kevin •   • b) flashlight

❸ James •   • c) lip balm

❹ Ruby •   • d) firesteel

B Fill in each blank with the right word below.

for	toward	around	on

❶ They all looked _____________, but they couldn't see anything because of the fog.

❷ They smeared lip balm _____________ the coat filling.

❸ They dragged branches _____________ a tree trunk.

❹ Boil the water over the fire and keep it boiling _____________ five minutes.

 Choose the best answer to each question.

❶ Why didn't the children blow the whistle as soon as they got lost?

a) They couldn't find the whistle.

b) They had forgotten the international distress signal.

c) They didn't want to appear to be babies.

d) They didn't think anyone was around to hear it.

❷ Where did Ruby get her foot stuck?

a) in a bog

b) in a rabbit hole

c) in a fence

d) in the river

D Which two words need to exchange places to make each sentence correct? Underline them.

> So the next <u>water</u> was to find some <u>task</u>.

❶ They could make a good place to camp and find a fire.

❷ Kevin tapped and smiled Ruby on the shoulder.

❸ The stars could see a few girls in the sky.

❹ The firesteel was no use and cotton wool without petroleum jelly.

A Daring Rescue

"Vanessa?" cried Ruby.

"Are you all right?"

There was a groan from somewhere below, in the shadows.

Ruby didn't think twice.

"I'm coming down," she said.

She tucked the flashlight into her belt.

It pointed downward.

She took a deep breath and lowered herself over the rocky edge.

KEY WORDS

- daring
- rescue
- somewhere
- shadow
- twice
- come down
- point
- downward
- take a deep breath
- lower oneself (*cf.* lower)
- rocky

Her dad had taught her to climb when she was younger.
Now, she tried to remember everything that she had
learned. **Aha!**

"Keep three points of contact with the rock," she told
herself.

"Two hands and a foot, or two feet and a hand.
Just move one at a time."

Slowly, carefully, she descended.

- **teach** (teach-taught-taught)
- **younger**
- **contact**
- **tell oneself**
- **feet**

- **move**
- **at a time**
- **descend**
- **shaky**
- **hurt**

- **bleed**
- **broken**
- **in reply**
- **thunder**
- **loud**

"Vanessa?" she called.

"I'm here," said Vanessa in a shaky voice.

"Are you hurt? Can you climb?"

"My head's bleeding and my glasses are broken.

My legs are OK, but I can't climb. I'm too scared."

Together, they shouted for help.

But they heard nothing in reply.

They thought nobody could hear them because the

thunder of the water below them was too loud.

"It's OK, Vanessa," said Ruby.

"We can do this together."

Slowly, carefully, the girls scrambled back up the side of the waterfall.

The moonlight shone on the wet rock.

Ruby had to take Vanessa's hands and feet and put them in the right places.

All the time, she heard the crashing of water below her and hoped that she wouldn't fall.

At last, the two girls reached the top.

James and Kevin were there to pull them up.

They had heard the cries after all.

Vanessa was soaking wet.
She was shivering, and her teeth
began to chatter.
"Let's get her nearer to the fire,"
said Ruby.
"She might get hypothermia." 
Together, they helped Vanessa
toward the fire and the shelter.

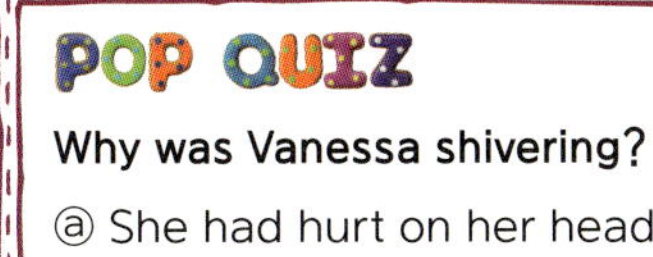

POP QUIZ

Why was Vanessa shivering?

ⓐ She had hurt on her head.
ⓑ She was wet.

KEY WORDS

- scramble
- moonlight
- shine (shine-shone-shone)
- crash
- hope

- soaking wet (*cf.* soak)
- shiver
- teeth
- chatter
- hypothermia

"We need to get her wet clothes off," said Ruby.

She helped Vanessa to undress.

Then, she gave Vanessa her own fleecy jacket.

James picked up the survival bag.

Vanessa got inside it, and Ruby got in as well.

She lay as close to Vanessa as she could.

She wrapped her arms around Vanessa.

Ruby's body heat and the warmth of the fire helped to warm Vanessa.

She stopped shivering.

Kevin tapped Ruby on the shoulder as though he wanted to tell her something.

"What is it?" she asked.

In reply, he picked up a twig and scratched a message in the dirt.

Get help, it said.

He gave her a thumbs-up signal, then hurried away through the trees. 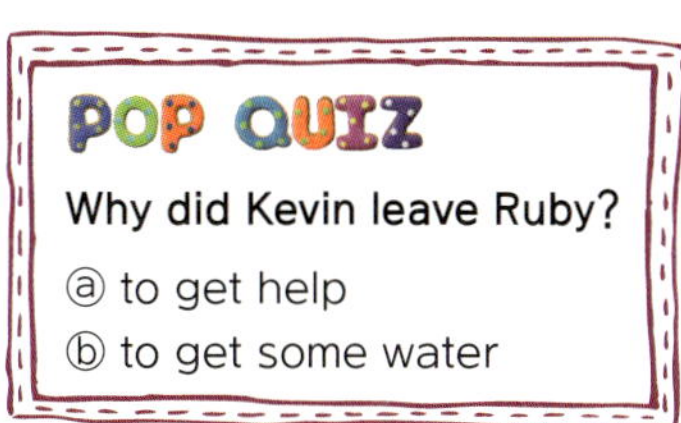

KEY WORDS

- undress (↔ dress)
- own
- fleecy
- pick up
- get inside[in]
- as well
- lie (lie-lay-lain)
- as + *Adjective / Adverb* + as + A can
- wrap

- body heat
- warm
- stop + *Verb*-ing
- twig
- scratch
- dirt
- get help
- hurry away

Vanessa began to cry.

"I'm sorry for being so horrible to you," she sobbed.

"I'm never normally like that."

"So why were you?"

Ruby felt sorry for Vanessa now.

"Everyone is always mean to me at school.

I wanted things to be different, just for a weekend.

I wanted to see how it felt."

Ruby smiled.

"How did it feel?"

"Horrible," snorted Vanessa.

"It's much nicer when we work together." Aha!

The girls and James gazed into the crackling fire.

They drifted into a light sleep.

Ruby stirred when she heard adult voices, shouting.

"We're over here!" she yelled.

Moments later, Holly and Major Matthews came rushing through the trees.

Kevin ran ahead of them, leading the way.

"Thank goodness we've found you!" gasped Holly.

"Everyone's out looking for you."

POP QUIZ

Who was leading the way for the adults?

ⓐ Kevin ⓑ Holly

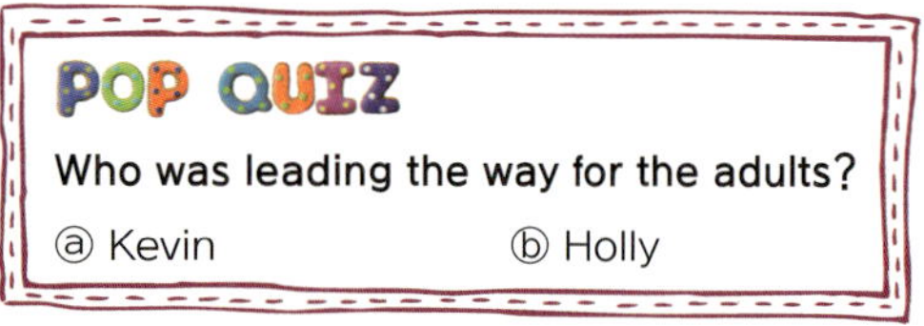

KEY WORDS

- moments later (*cf.* moment)
- run ahead of
- lead the way
- thank goodness

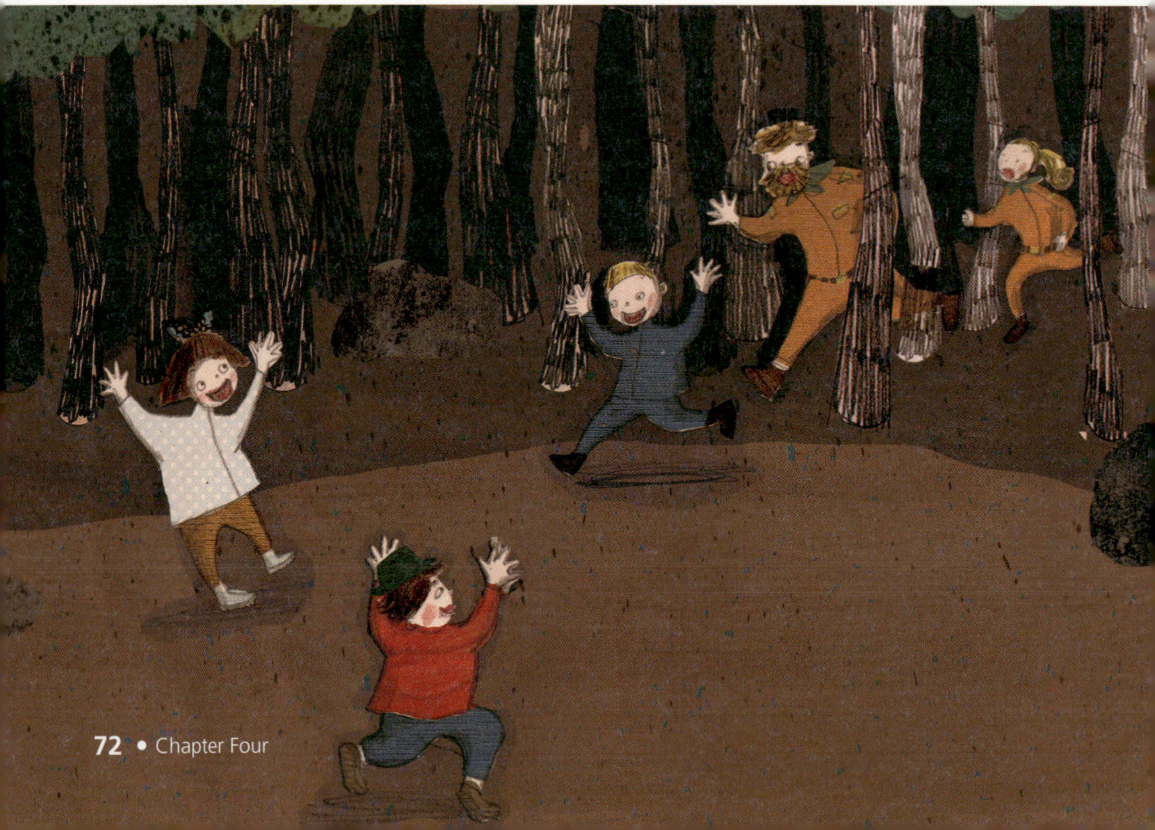

"How did you find us?" asked Ruby.

"Kevin found a lookout on the edge of a cliff," explained Holly.

"He lit a fire there as a signal.

We saw it in the dark.

I couldn't believe it when I realized that you were on Survivor's Peak.

We walked toward the light and found Kevin there, making the fire as big as possible."

- lookout
- dark
- as + *Adjective / Adverb* + as possible

Kevin smiled and nodded his head.

"I thought you were an idiot, Kevin," admitted Vanessa.

She reached out and took hold of his hand.

"How wrong I was!" **Aha!**

"I think we've all been wrong about a lot of things,"
said Ruby.

A walkie-talkie on Major Matthews' belt crackled.

"Come on," he said.

"We're taking all of you back to the center.

Warm beds for everyone, I think!"

Vanessa and Ruby looked at each other.

"I think," Ruby said slowly, "that it would be fun to stay

out here."

"Vanessa can't stay," said the major.

"She's been injured."

"Only minor cuts and bruises," said Holly.

"I've brought a first-aid kit.

I'll fix her up."

"I'm fine now," said Vanessa.

"I'm lovely and warm, too."

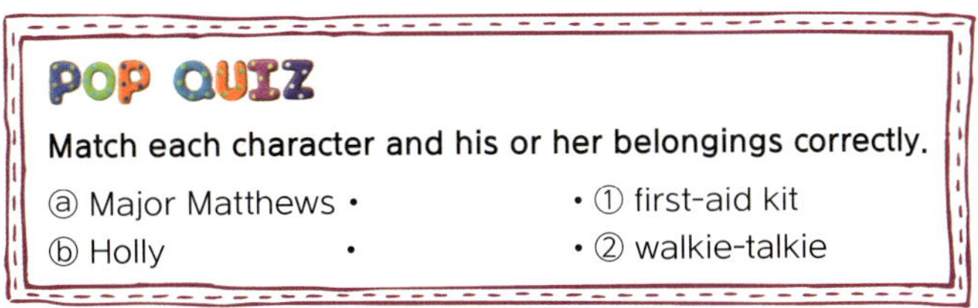

KEY WORDS

- walkie-talkie
- each other
- stay out
- injured (*cf.* injure)
- minor
- cut
- bruise
- bring (bring-brought-brought)
- first-aid kit
- fix up
- fine
- lovely

"You can't take her back without us," protested Ruby.
"We started out as a team and we want to stay as a team."

"I know," said Holly.

"Let's go back down to the safe area, inside the fence. You can set up a camp there, and I'll take Vanessa back to the center for some more treatment.
Then, if she feels well enough, she can come and join you for the rest of the night.
I'll stay, too."

Major Matthews looked doubtful.

"Please?" begged Ruby.

"We know how to make a fire and a good shelter." **Aha!**

Major Matthews shook his head, but he was smiling at the same time.

"All right," he said.

"You deserve it."

"After all," said Ruby, "we survived Survivor's Peak!"

KEY WORDS

- start out
- treatment
- the rest of

- doubtful
- beg
- at the same time

- deserve
- survive

SURVI
BAC
super

Chapter Four Comprehension Quiz

A Fill in each blank with the right word below.

scrambled	wrapped	helped	picked

❶ The girls _____________ back up the side of the waterfall.

❷ Together, they _____________ Vanessa toward the fire and the shelter.

❸ James _____________ up the survival bag.

❹ Ruby _____________ her arms around Vanessa.

B Circle the correct word for each underlined part.

❶ I wanted things to be (<u>different</u> / <u>diferent</u>), just for a weekend.

❷ "I (<u>thoght</u> / <u>thought</u>) you were an idiot, Kevin," admitted Vanessa.

❸ "Only (<u>miner</u> / <u>minor</u>) cuts and bruises," said Holly.

❹ "I'm fine now," said Vanessa. "I'm (<u>lovely</u> / <u>lovley</u>) and warm, too."

C Choose the best answer to each question.

❶ Who got inside the survival bag?

a) Ruby and James

b) James and Vanessa

c) Ruby and Vanessa

d) just Vanessa

❷ What woke Ruby from her light sleep?

a) thunder of the water

b) Kevin's voice, whispering

c) a crackling fire

d) adult voices, shouting

D Mark T for true or F for false.

❶ Vanessa put Ruby's hands and feet in the right places. T F

❷ The moon was shining that night. T F

❸ James and Kevin pulled the girls up at the top. T F

❹ Ruby gave Vanessa her waterproof coat. T F

Let's Review the Story

Fill in the blanks to review the story.

Title: Lost in the __________

Characters

- R________, V________, J________, and K________ (children)
- H________, M________ M________, D________ (adults)

Chapter 1

- Ruby arrives at Oakfield A________ Center and meets V________, who is rude to her.
- Ruby is put into a t________ with Vanessa, James, and Kevin.

Chapter 2

- The teams learn how to make a f________, how to build a s________, and how to n________.
- Then, they are given instructions and things for s________ to spend the night o________ in a safe area.

Chapter 3

- The team leaves the s________ area and gets lost on S________ P________.
- They make a s________ and a f________, but when they search for w________, Vanessa falls down a cliff beside a waterfall.

Chapter 4

- Ruby rescues Vanessa but she is c________ and i________.
- Kevin makes a f________ to call for help.
- H________ and Major M________ find the children. They decide that they want to stay o________ after all!

Let's Think & Talk

Think about the following questions and answer them freely.

❶ Do you like outdoor activities like the survival training camp in the story? Tell us your opinion about whether this kind of activity is needed for children your age or not.

❷ If you were going hiking or camping, what survival tools would you bring to protect against danger? Pick three things that you think you would need and tell us the reason.

❸ Have you ever teamed up with your friends for an activity? Tell us what you did as a team member, how you felt about the activity, and what you experienced.

Let's Review the Story

Title: Lost in the **Forest**

Characters
- **Ruby**, **Vanessa**, **James**, and **Kevin** (children)
- **Holly**, **Major** **Matthews**, **Dad** (adults)

Chapter 1
- Ruby arrives at Oakfield **Adventure** Center and meets **Vanessa**, who is rude to her.
- Ruby is put into a **team** with Vanessa, James, and Kevin.

Chapter 2
- The teams learn how to make a **fire**, how to build a **shelter**, and how to **navigate**.
- Then, they are given instructions and things for **survival** to spend the night **outdoors** in a safe area.

Chapter 3
- The team leaves the **safe** area and gets lost on **Survivor's Peak**.
- They make a **shelter** and a **fire**, but when they search for **water**, Vanessa falls down a cliff beside a waterfall.

Chapter 4
- Ruby rescues Vanessa but she is **cold** and **injured**.
- Kevin makes a **fire** to call for help.
- **Holly** and Major **Matthews** find the children. They decide that they want to stay **outside** after all!

Come and
get me.
It's horrible
here.

- **Lost in the Forest**
- **Level 3**
- **27 Questions**

  (Vocabulary 6 / Reading Comprehension 16/

  Sentence Structure & Grammar 5)

1. Which of the following explains the meaning of "descend" best?
   ① to listen
   ② to rescue
   ③ to move upward
   ④ to move downward

2. What does "flammable" mean in the following sentence?

   Petroleum jelly is "flammable."

   ① sticky
   ② rocky
   ③ producing oxygen
   ④ catches fire easily

3. Which of the following has the wrong past tense form of the verb?
   ① lay − laid
   ② light − lought
   ③ drink − drank
   ④ bend − bent

4. Which of the following has the same meaning as the sentence below?

   James nodded reluctantly.

   ① He was happy when he nodded.
   ② He nodded very fast.
   ③ He didn't really want to nod.
   ④ He thought about it first before he nodded.

※ Choose the right word for each blank. (5~6)

5.

> If they do burn, they will ___________ a lot of smoke.

① press
② protest
③ explain
④ produce

6.

> Ruby got her foot ___________ in a sticky, muddy bog.

① pulled
② stuck
③ convinced
④ stepped

7. Why did Dad think the weekend's activity would be good for Ruby?
① He thought that she wasn't confident enough.
② He thought that she didn't get outside enough.
③ He thought that she needed to meet more people.
④ He thought that she spent too much time shopping.

8. How did Survivor's Peak get its name?
① Nobody had ever managed to climb it.
② Everyone who had climbed it had died.
③ Only one person had survived in a team of climbers.
④ It was named after the person who had first discovered it.

9. How had people died on Survivor's Peak?
   ① People had died of hypothermia.
   ② People had slipped into ice caves.
   ③ People had fallen down steep cliffs.
   ④ People had drunk dirty water.

10. To whom did Ruby try to send a text?
    ① Mom
    ② Dad
    ③ Holly
    ④ Vanessa

11. Why were green sticks NOT suitable for the fire?
    ① They would burn too easily.
    ② They would break too easily.
    ③ They would not burn easily.
    ④ They would not produce smoke easily.

12. Why did Holly say that Vanessa needed to work with the children as a team?
    ① Her life could depend on it.
    ② It would make her life easier.
    ③ She would win a prize at the end of the day.
    ④ She would get sent home if she didn't work with the other children.

13. Which of these is NOT part of the fire triangle?

① fuel

② heat

③ water

④ oxygen

14. What did the children use to light their fire?

① a match

② a firesteel

③ a compass

④ a burning piece of paper

15. What did the children use to build their shelter?

① branches

② rocks

③ leaves

④ earth

16. What did Major Matthews tell the children to use in an emergency?

① a fire

② a whistle

③ a flashlight

④ a cell phone

17. Why did Vanessa climb over the fence?
    ① She thought that it was the way to the first checkpoint.
    ② She didn't know that it marked the edge of the safe area.
    ③ She wanted to do survival training without any adults around.
    ④ She knew that there was a good place to camp on the other side.

18. Why did James take his backpack off?
    ① to help Ruby
    ② to light a fire
    ③ to get a drink
    ④ to put on a waterproof coat

19. Why did Vanessa offer to go and look for water?
    ① She had found a river on the map.
    ② She did not trust anyone else to find the water.
    ③ She thought she could hear better than anyone else.
    ④ She thought that it was her fault that they were lost.

20. Why had Vanessa been mean to Ruby?
    ① She was jealous of Ruby.
    ② Ruby had been mean to her.
    ③ Other people had been mean to her.
    ④ Ruby had been mean to James and Kevin.

21. How could Kevin ask adults for help?
   ① He had blown the whistle.
   ② He had used a walkie-talkie.
   ③ He had walked back to the center.
   ④ He had lit a fire on the edge of a cliff.

22. Why did Major Matthews think that Vanessa should NOT camp out overnight?
   ① She had an injury.
   ② She did not follow the instructions.
   ③ She was not a good team member.
   ④ She had been unkind to other people.

※ Choose the wrong part of each sentence. (23~26)

23. There <u>must</u> <u>have</u> <u>be</u> around twenty children there, but they <u>made</u>
       ①   ②   ③   ④
   enough noise for a hundred.

24. James <u>carried</u> a <u>fourth</u> <u>backpack</u>.
       ①   ②   ③   ④

25.
It's very nicer when we work together.
①　②　③　　④

26.
Now, she tried to remember everything what she had learned.
　　　①　②　　　③　　　　　　　　　　④

27. What is the correct sentence?

① Ruby was putted with two boys called James and Kevin.

② Ruby was put with two boys called James and Kevin.

③ Ruby putted with two boys called James and Kevin.

④ Ruby have be put with two boys called James and Kevin.

Memo

Memo 

Sarah J. Dodd

Sarah J. Dodd is an experienced primary school teacher who resides in the UK, but has also lived and taught in Australia. She has a PhD in Science and a certificate in Creative Writing. She has published several books for children: "An Angel Anyway" (Anyway Press, 2008), the "Little Angels" series (Lion Children's Books, 2009/10), "The Lion Picture Bible" (Lion Children's Books, 2015) and "Legs: the tale of a meerkat lost and found" (Lion Children's Books, 2015). Her poetry for children has also been highly commended and published in the anthology "Let in the Stars" (Manchester Metropolitan University, 2014).
She is currently working on further picture books for the very young, and a novel for older children.

Lost in the Forest

Written by Sarah J. Dodd
Illustrated by Jiyeong Kim

First Published in March 2017

Editorial Manager: Juyon Choi
Editors: Juyon Choi, Kyunghee Jang, Jiyeong Park
Designers: Eunhee Lee, Elim
Cover Designer: Eunhee Lee

Published and distributed by

Darakwon Bldg., 64-1 Jandari-ro, Mapo-gu, Seoul, Korea 04031
Tel: 82-2-736-2031(ext. 250)   Fax: 82-2-732-2037
Homepage: www.ihappyhouse.co.kr
Publisher: Kyudo Chung

ISBN: 978-89-6653-508-8 18740 / 978-89-6653-156-1 18740(set)

[Components]
• 1 Audio CD (Recording Studio: Aram)
• Answer Keys & Korean Translation: Free download at www.ihappyhouse.co.kr